my feelings

activity book

The Mother Company Presents

RUBY'S STUDIO

Social & Emotional Learning For Kids

Created by:
Abbie Schiller & Samantha Kurtzman-Counter
Book Design by:
Rae Friis

WCP&Printing - Stevens Point, WI - USA - October 2011 - 1st Printing

About The Author
{that's you!}

My name is:_____

I am _____ YEARS old & _____ FEET _____ INCHES tall

My BIRTHDAY is:_____

My EYE color is:_____ {color here} & HAIR color is:_____

My nickname is:_____

My ADDRESS is:_____

My favorite COLOR is:_____

I like to EAT:_____

My FAVORITE thing to do is:_____

★ ★ ★

paste a photo or draw a picture of yourself

p. 3

About My Family

I LIVE with:_____

The other PEOPLE in my family are:_____

_____

I have (circle) 0 1 2 3 4 5 pets. Their names are:_____

I LAUGH really hard when someone in my family:

_____

I get really MAD when someone in my family:_____

_____

I LOVE it when someone in my family:_____

_____

MY FAVORITE thing to do with my family is:_____

What makes my family SPECIAL is:_____

_____

p. 4

About My Home

I LIVE in: _____. (city or town where you live)

That's in: _____. (state or country where you live)

The AREA I live in is a (circle one):   big city   small town   countryside   island   suburb

homeward bound!

I have: MY OWN room.

I SHARE a room with: _____.

I GO TO (circle one): preschool   elementary school   daycare   homeschool   not in school yet

I GET THERE by (circle one):

car   bike   walk   skip   skate   crawl   bus

The place I go that makes me MOST HAPPY is: _____

When I feel sad, the place I LIKE TO GO is: _____

If I could go ANYWHERE I wanted, it would be: _____

BECAUSE: _____

The Feelings I've Felt

{Circle all the feelings you've ever felt}

happy frustrated proud shy

scared sad jealous thankful

mad confused annoyed worried

hopeful embarrassed lonely surprised

OTHER feelings you've had: _____.

Today's Date: _____ & Time: _____

DRAW A PICTURE OF YOURSELF THAT SHOWS HOW YOU FEEL RIGHT NOW.

{or fill the circle in with a color that shows how you feel right now}

How I feel right now: _____

PROUD

{place
PROUD
sticker
here}

WRITE OR DRAW WHAT MAKES YOU PROUD ABOVE

WHEN I FEEL PROUD I...

Circle and color the images that are true for you!

feel good about myself

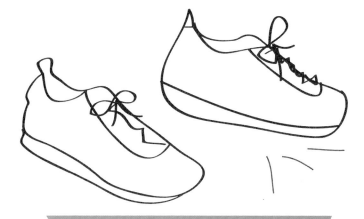

jump up & down

flex my muscles

tell everyone I know

FRUSTRATED

{place
FRUSTRATED
sticker
here}

WRITE OR DRAW WHAT MAKES YOU FRUSTRATED ABOVE

WHEN I FEEL FRUSTRATED I...

Circle and color the images that are true for you!

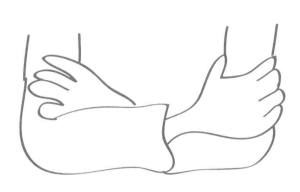

cross my arms

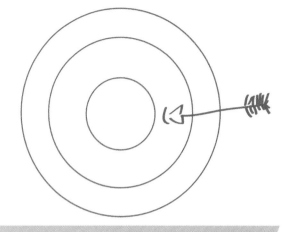

want to give up

want to yell (and sometimes do)

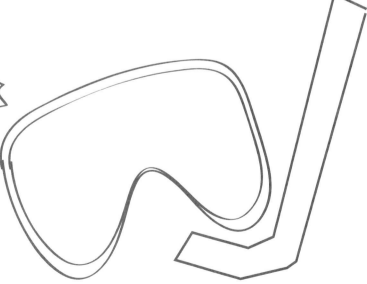

take a breath
& try again

p. 11

SHY

{place SHY sticker here}

WRITE OR DRAW WHAT MAKES YOU SHY ABOVE

WHEN I FEEL SHY I...

Circle and color the images that are true for you!

want to hide

feel tiny

get really quiet

just wave to say hello

P. 13

HOW MY FEELINGS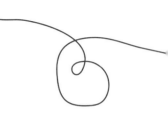

INSTRUCTIONS...

Pick a feeling from column A and figure out what you might do in column B to change it into a new feeling in column C.

*** HINT ***
It can work a bunch of different ways!

A. When I feel...

MAD

SAD

FRUSTRATED

scared

SHY

JEALOUS

I feel PROUD when...

I feel SAD when...

I feel SHY when...

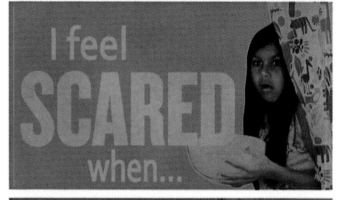

I feel SCARED when...

I feel FRUSTRATED when...

I feel HAPPY when...

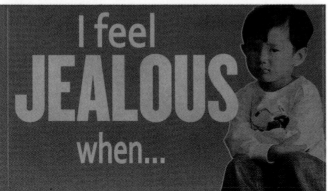

I feel JEALOUS when...

I feel MAD when...

CHANGE...

B. I know I can...

C. And then I feel...

STOMP MY FEET	CALM
CRY	RELIEVED
TAKE A DEEP BREATH	HAPPY
tell someone	confident
TAKE IT SLOW	PROUD
KEEP TRYING	LOVED

JEALOUS

{place
JEALOUS
sticker
here}

WRITE OR DRAW WHAT MAKES YOU JEALOUS ABOVE

WHEN I FEEL JEALOUS I...

Circle and color the images that are true for you!

feel like nothing is fair

want someone to pay attention to me

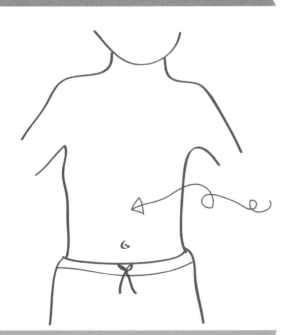

feel tight in my tummy

try to remember I'm special

SCARED

{place SCARED sticker here}

WRITE OR DRAW WHAT MAKES YOU SCARED ABOVE

WHEN I FEEL SCARED I...

Circle and color the images that are true for you!

feel my heart pounding

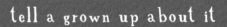

tell a grown up about it

go someplace safe

squeeze my lovey tight

Circle your answers and color in the picture below

When my friends are sad, I............ {circle any that are true for you}

Ask what's wrong

Give them some space

See if I can help

Give them a hug

Feel sad too

Have you ever made someone feel better when he/she was sad?
If so, what did you do?

_____

My Surprised Face

Look in the mirror and make a surprised face.
Draw what that face looks like in the mirror below.
(*Or draw something with a color that reminds you of surprised feelings*)

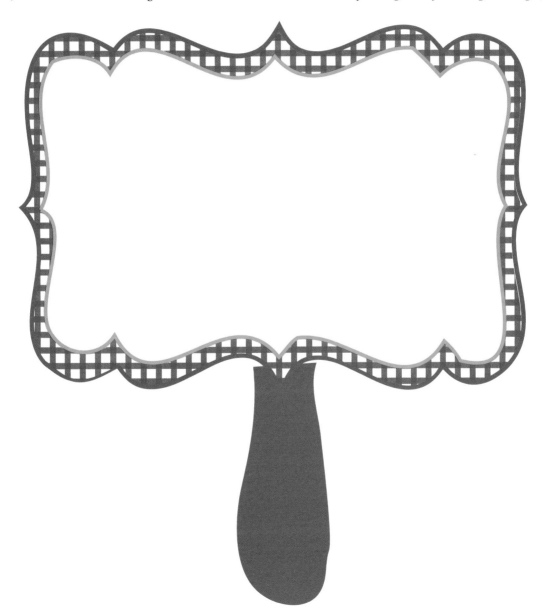

P. 21

MAD

{place MAD sticker here}

WRITE OR DRAW WHAT MAKES YOU MAD ABOVE

WHEN I FEEL MAD I...

Circle and color the images that are true for you!

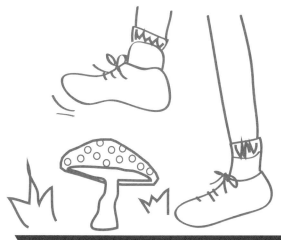

stomp my feet

ARGH!!

go outside & yell

That's not OK with me

Please stop

I don't like it when you do that

try to find words to talk about it

take a deep breath & count to 10

SAD

{place
SAD
sticker
here}

WRITE OR DRAW WHAT MAKES YOU SAD ABOVE

WHEN I FEEL SAD I...

Circle & color the images that are true for you!

cry

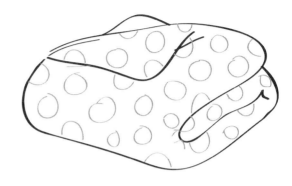

snuggle with an animal
or blanket

want a hug

talk about it with
someone who loves me

HAPPY

{place HAPPY sticker here}

WRITE OR DRAW WHAT MAKES YOU HAPPY ABOVE

WHEN I FEEL HAPPY I...

Circle and color the images that are true for you!

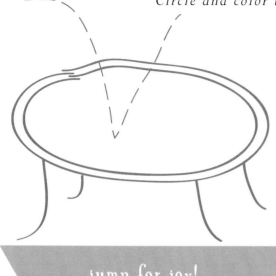

jump for joy!

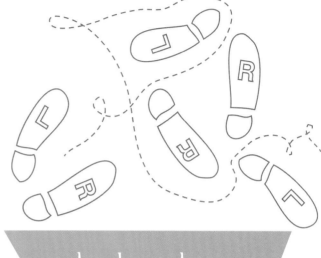

do a happy dance

hoot! hoot!

smile & laugh

play & play & play!

What Makes Me Special

I am (circle all that are true for you):

silly   smart   strong   clumsy   quiet   creative

curious   considerate _____(fill in the blank)

People tell me they LOVE ME because I:_____

_____

When they say that, I FEEL:_____

_____

When I feel love for someone else, I SHOW IT by:_____

_____

you are
LOVED

The most IMPORTANT thing to me is:_____

Mostly, I feel_____TO BE ME!